BASICS

URBAN BUILDING
BLOCKS

\\ THORSTEN BÜRKLIN \\ MICHAEL PETEREK

BASICS

URBAN BUILDING BLOCKS

BIRKHÄUSER
BASEL · BOSTON · BERLIN

CONTENTS

FOREWORD

Buildings do not emerge in isolation but as part of a natural or built environment. This environment can consist of a web of historical, cultural and landscape relations, but in today's world, designs are implemented and architecture emerges primarily in an urban context. A large-scale urban project can be designed on the drawing board and built as a coherent unit if the city's growth potential warrants this approach, but urban planners and architects generally create designs for cities that have evolved over generations and are the products of different influences and ideologies. Despite this complexity, we find recurring "building blocks" that shape and influence the urban environment.

The field of "urban planning" in the *Basics* series provides students with a practical, instructive introduction to the foundations of urban design. The present book describes typical urban building blocks and their features in order to give students a basic understanding of the fundamental structure and design of cities. It elucidates the row, block, courtyard, arcade, ribbon, solitaire, group and shed, focusing on structural principles, functional possibilities and cultural historical backgrounds. Knowledge of the elements used to design cities is important for the analytical and creative work in urban planning, regardless of whether the goal is to create new urban environments, add to or renew existing urban structures, or to design individual buildings in an urban area.

Bert Bielefeld
Editor

INTRODUCTION:
FROM INDIVIDUAL BUILDING TO BUILDING BLOCK
OF THE CITY

The city is more than the sum of its individual buildings. It is also more than "large-scale architecture". In its neighbourhoods and quarters – the arenas of our day-to-day lives – it is made up of built structural elements that mediate between the scale of the individual architectural objects and that of larger units such as neighbourhoods or even entire urban districts. These elements thus mediate between the individuality (and privacy) of a house and plot of land and the collective (and public) sphere of a more comprehensive urban environment.

These structural elements can also be termed "building blocks of the city". They can appear as different forms and geometries in the urban layout: rows, blocks, courtyards, arcades, ribbons, solitaires, groups and "sheds". Naturally, diverse combinations can be imagined and are already part of urban reality. By virtue of their special form and unique combinations, they influence the way we live together by promoting certain functions and lifestyles and hindering others. Knowledge of these building blocks is therefore an essential aspect of the craft of urban design. Urban planners and architects must grapple with them in order to evaluate the effects that their designs will have. It is only by understanding these urban elements – which differ greatly in terms of form, function, size and significance – that they can responsibly design cities.

The following chapters present these building blocks from different perspectives, focusing on their spatial structure and design, functional objectives, integration into the urban environment, the associated differentiation of private and public areas, and the conditions under which they emerge. Where relevant, the chapters also touch on the way these basic structural elements of the city have changed over the years. Individual observations are illustrated using historical and modern examples.

Each building block is discussed in relation to the following four points:

_ Form and spatial structure (physical description of the urban element)
_ Formation of urban space (the impact of the "building block" and the significance it has for its surroundings and for urban space)

_ Functions, orientation and access
_ Historical examples

Of course the distinctions between these building blocks are not always as clear in architectural and urban reality as the thematic structure of this book might suggest. There are a great many overlaps, borderline cases and "hybrids" that do not fall into a clearly definable category.

Even so, it is important that students first study the building blocks of the city in their purest form so that they can use this knowledge to analyse the different combinations and hybrid forms found in cities and take them into account sufficiently in their designs. With this in mind, this book aims to provide formal, functional and organizational information and knowledge concerning the individual building blocks of the city.

THE ROW

The row is one of the oldest and most important structural elements in cities and settlements. It joins together individual plots of land and buildings along a straight, angular or curved line, formed and accessed by the street. It creates a broader urban planning context that extends beyond the individual building. The basic spatial structure of large areas of our cities and villages consists of rows.

FORM AND SPATIAL STRUCTURE

Relation to the
street

Constitutive of the row is that the buildings' entrances and access paths are oriented toward the street, which defines the row spatially and functionally. › Fig. 1

Development
forms

In addition to the principle of linear addition, rows can have entirely different development forms. They can be open or closed (i.e. terraces), and have one or two sides. In open rows of single-family or semi-detached homes, there is open space surrounding the buildings. Whereas single-family homes have open space on all four sides, each semi-detached house is joined to its twin on one side. In terraces, there are no gaps between the buildings, which form a continuous visible spatial edge.

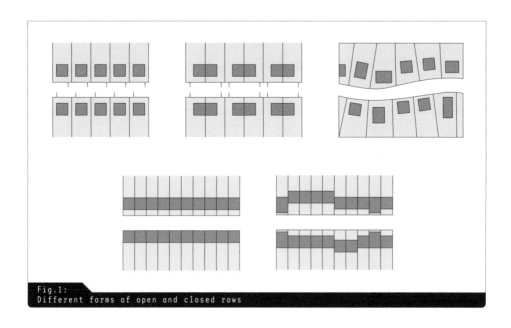

Fig.1:
Different forms of open and closed rows

Fig.2:
One-sided row on a slope in Bath in the south of England

In a one-sided row (which can be either open or closed), only one side of the street is developed; a two-sided row has buildings on both sides. The buildings on opposite sides of a two-sided row need not necessarily be identical. The two sides of the row are formally independent of each other. The row, particularly in its open form, can be excellently adapted to dynamic site topographies. › Fig. 2

Diversity in unity

The row is a highly flexible urban building block and allows for diverse formal principles. The appearance, three-dimensional form (width, depth, height) and functions of the individual buildings in a row can be similar or even absolutely identical. › Fig. 3 They can also differ significantly in appearance, with highly differentiated, irregular or heterogeneous forms. › Fig. 4 This means that each individual building can have a distinct appearance and identity.

Even so, rows in an urban context are often arranged so that the individual parts are in harmony. The reasons are primarily economic: the repeated use of the same prototype facilitates the quick and inexpensive construction of buildings and apartments. Single-family, semi-detached or terraced houses that emerge in this fashion – each with the same size and the same internal and external form – leave their mark on the character of an entire area.

In theory, the row can be continued lengthwise ad infinitum. However, infrastructure capacity and long distances place limitations on row

Fig.3:
Row of identical houses in the Royal
Circus, Bath

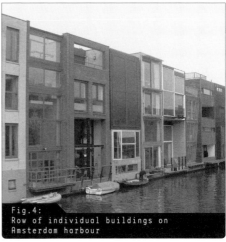

Fig.4:
Row of individual buildings on
Amsterdam harbour

length since at some point site development becomes uneconomical. Furthermore, long rows make it impossible to develop the entire depth of the plots behind the buildings as building land. Diagonal streets must be introduced to break up the rows and create more economical urban units in the form of blocks. › Chapter The city block

Economic efficiency is another reason why one-sided rows are usually an exception in urban planning. If a row has two sides, twice as many buildings can be linked to the urban infrastructure with the same expenditure of money and effort. One-sided rows are generally confined to special areas such as the edge of housing estates or the area along parks and rivers, where there is a need for particularly high-quality residential and working space.

FORMATION OF URBAN SPACE

Through their direct link to the street, rows form clear and distinguishable urban spaces. At the same time, they are integrated into the infrastructure network of the entire city, and thus become part of a cohesive urban spatial web. Rows can flexibly fill gaps and intermediate spaces in this urban structure, and they can also be easily connected to other urban elements such as city blocks, ribbons or solitaires.

Front and back   Due to their orientation toward the street, rows are characterized by a clear spatial demarcation between front and rear. This distinction is

13

reflected not only in the different functions (public use on the street side, and private or collective use in the gardens or courtyards), but also in different architectural designs. On the street side, the buildings usually have a more restrained and stately design, while in the rear they may be less regimented and more influenced by significant processes of individual appropriation and alteration (e.g. extensions and remodelling to create terraces, pergolas, winter gardens and roof space).

Transition to
street space

The design of the front area facing the street is of great importance for the formation of urban space. This is especially true of the transition from the private space of the building to the public space of the city. Depending on location, orientation, topography, type of building and other factors, this front transitional area can be designed in a variety of ways. In densely developed historical cities, it was once common practice to construct buildings directly on public streets in order to save space. Property boundaries and building lines coincided. This continues to be a suitable solution today if the ground floor of a building is used for commercial purposes, but it is not effective for residential uses because pedestrians are able to look into private spaces if the ground floor is on the same level as the street. In the residential neighbourhoods of most modern cities, architects therefore usually create a deep buffer zone between the private area of the building and public space. This can take the form of a planted strip of land, a front garden or a private front courtyard that provides space for important supplementary functions next to the house (parking spaces, carports, storage space for bikes, rubbish bins, places to relax, sitting areas, terraces etc.). Even a row of trees can serve as a transitional area. By slightly raising the ground floor level, architects can keep passers-by from looking into the house and also provide residents with an attractive view of street space from inside the apartment. > Fig. 5

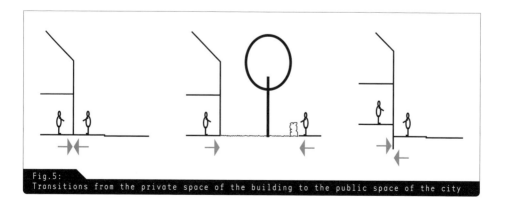

Fig.5:
Transitions from the private space of the building to the public space of the city

FUNCTIONS, ORIENTATION AND ACCESS

Combined uses

Because of its direct link to the network of urban streets and city infrastructure, the row can perform the full gamut of an urban building block's functions. Even today, we find vivid examples of mixed uses in the streets that make up historical city centres and in organically evolved neighbourhoods. The ground floors in row developments are especially well suited to uses beyond mere housing (shops, restaurants and small businesses). If required, these functions can be extended to the rear of the property by means of extensions or additional auxiliary buildings – common practice in closed rows that otherwise offer little space. Entrance drives through the front buildings can be helpful since they provide access to the rear area of the plot even for cars. Yet they subject the quiet, private area protected from the street to additional disturbances from the cars driving in, noise and greater public accessibility.

That said, the row has developed into a primarily monofunctional urban element that is mostly used for housing. This is the result of modern urban planning concepts that, in line with the Athens Charter, separate urban functions into housing, work and transport.

> 🏠

Dense terraced
housing

Rows formed by closed groups of terraced houses became popular in the 20th century, particularly because they made economical use of the limited land available for urban expansion. Due to its capacity to encompass a large number of subdivisions, the row allows for individual housing solutions on private plots that are characterized by a high degree of development density, compared to the open rows of single-family or semi-detached homes found elsewhere. In addition to the economic efficiency of standardized building elements, the row offers the advantage of saved space and costs since the individual homes can be built on very narrow pieces of property.

> 🏠

🏠

\\ Note:
The Athens Charter was passed in 1933 at the fourth meeting of the Congrès Internationaux d'Architecture Moderne (International Congress of Modern Architecture). The conference was held in July and August 1933 on board the "Patris" sailing from Marseilles to Athens. Le Corbusier was most important initiator and main author of the Charter.

🏠

\\ Note:
The width of the plots used for terraced housing usually measures 5.5 to 6.5 m. In some cases, these plots can be as narrow as 4.5 m. If they have a depth of 25 to 30 m, the total surface area is 150 to 180 m^2. By contrast, semi-detached and single-family homes usually require plots of 300 to 400 m^2 or more.

Since rows are built along streets, their orientation in relation to the points of the compass and the sun depends on the course of the street. As a consequence, natural and artificial lighting conditions for the houses and apartments may vary greatly with property orientation. Any such locational disadvantages must be compensated for by adequate floor plan design (e.g. floor plans that use both sides of the building), since rows, particularly closed ones, receive sunlight only at certain times of the day.

> ◧

One special form of terraced housing involves stacking one row on top of the other. This usually involves two duplexes, with the upper unit accessed via an outdoor corridor. This solution can be used to create a high-density urban environment that has the same residential quality and atmosphere offered by separately accessed individual homes. › Fig. 6

Recently, the term "townhouse" has come to describe buildings in a row (or on a block) that combine the functions of housing and work in a densely developed inner-city area. › Fig. 7 Townhouses are at least three storeys tall and sometimes four. They offer sufficient space for a supplementary commercial use (e.g. a store or an office on the ground floor), and they might also have a (separate) granny flat, a private courtyard or a garden. Some feature additional outdoor space such as a roof terrace. Townhouses are characterized by great architectural diversity and individuality.

◧

\\ Note:
Rows facing east or west receive sufficient sunlight in the evening and the morning, but no direct midday sun. In the summer, the sunlight can heat up the rooms and make it necessary to install sunshades on the buildings. Rows oriented north or south in the northern hemisphere benefit from sunlight coming from the south, which can create pleasant indoor temperatures particularly during the winter months. This orientation offers the added advantage of energy savings (passive solar energy use). However, it has the disadvantage that any rooms on the northern side of the building receive no sunlight at all during the day (with the exception of late afternoon sun at the peak of summer). This is why you should never design, say, a children's room with this orientation. Nevertheless, the northern side of a building is often better suited for studios and certain work spaces since people can work undisturbed if lighting conditions remain constant. It should be noted that such references to north-south orientations in this book should be reversed when considering buildings in the southern hemisphere.

Fig.6:
Stacked rows of duplexes in the
densely developed Margess Road estate
in London

Fig.7:
Rows of townhouses in the centre of
Karlsruhe

HISTORICAL EXAMPLES

The creation of rows made up of similar plots and buildings played an important role in the cities of Antiquity, including the newly founded colonies of ancient Greece. The reason for their popularity is that they offered a simple and rational principle for dividing up urban land. An additional advantage is that they made it possible to treat all residents equally (the same conditions and the same use for all).

Medieval
townhouses

The cities of the Middle Ages were also based on rows of plots and buildings. Although these buildings were identical in terms of typology, their architectural details were often quite different. The craftsman's or merchant's house, with its mixed uses, formed the basic unit of the city. In the front it meshed with the public space of the city – with its alleys, streets and squares. In the rear, it overlooked a completely private area consisting of courtyards and gardens that were almost invisible to the outer world. If the urban space was densely developed and more space was required, additional buildings could be built at the rear. Typical examples can be found in numerous medieval towns such as Gdansk, Lübeck and Amsterdam. Cities like these have managed to retain their urban atmosphere and quality of life up until today. › Fig. 8

Garden cities

Historical cities and, in particular, 19th-century industrial cities were criticized for being too densely developed and having cramped living conditions. In response to this, the garden city movement, which

Fig.8:
Rows of medieval merchants' houses in the old part of Gdansk

originated in England in the early 20th century, sought to create new residential estates and urban expansion projects that were modelled on open and closed rows. The urban planning and spatial objectives hinged on creating a diverse, open development structure and were linked to the intention to implement general reforms – social, economic, health and hygiene concerns. Urban planners were particularly keen to provide the poorly housed working class with dwellings in green areas. Deep gardens behind the terraced homes could be used agriculturally to meet the families' needs. › Fig. 9

› 🛈

Modern estates   These concepts also played a role in the design of terraced housing estates by the *Neues Bauen* movement in the early 20th century – as can be seen in the residential estates of Bruno Taut and Martin Wagner in Berlin

🛈

\\Note:
The central work of the garden city movement is *Tomorrow: A Peaceful Path to Real Reform* by Ebenezer Howard, published in 1898. Howard wanted the garden city to combine the advantages of both the city and the country. Since these cities were supposed to be places to live and work, they included both industrial and cultural facilities. According to Howard's concept, six largely autonomous cities (each with 32,000 residents) were grouped around a central urban area (with 58,000 residents). However, only a few of these autonomous garden cities were ever built. The first was Letchworth, founded north of London in 1904. Most were planned as garden suburbs on the peripheries of existing cities, upon which they remained functionally and economically dependent.

Fig.9:
Terraced houses in the Karlsruhe garden city suburb

Fig.10:
Terraced houses in Römerstadt, Frankfurt

and the projects built in Frankfurt am Main under Ernst May, director of the municipal planning office. The Römerstadt estate (1927–1928) is based on the principle of rowing together standardized, economically laid-out homes, each with its own garden. This arrangement creates a concise urban street space with a pleasant atmosphere. › Fig. 10

The current renaissance of townhouses shows that the row continues to have great appeal. It is an urban housing form with tremendous individuality that supports a variety of lifestyles. At the same time, the uncontrolled development of the areas surrounding our cities – a result of the construction of single-family homes that consume an inordinate amount of land – underscores the urgent need for sustainable housing models like the row that require less space.

\\ Note:
The *Neues Bauen* architectural movement emerged around the Bauhaus, a school that was opened in Weimar in 1919 with workshops for crafts, architecture and the visual arts. The movement's primary goal was to transcend historicism and create rational architecture that made use of industrial production methods.

THE CITY BLOCK

Like the row, the city block (or block of buildings) is one of the oldest and most important elements of urban design. From Antiquity onward, it has exerted a major influence on the structure of European cities. However, in the early 20th century, urban planners argued that it created inequitable living conditions, and it was not until the end of the century that its positive qualities as an urban element were rediscovered.

FORM AND SPATIAL STRUCTURE

Outside and
inside

The block consists of a group of plots – or, in special cases, of a single property – and it is surrounded and accessed by streets on all sides. The front facades of the buildings forming the block are oriented toward the street, creating a clear distinction between the block's interior and exterior space and a strong architectural orientation toward a front public area and a rear private realm. The block's interior may be left open or partially or fully covered with buildings. It may be used for gardens, courtyards, open areas, garages, storage spaces, ancillary buildings and so on.

Block
geometries

Blocks can have a wide range of geometries. They can be triangular, rectangular, square, polygonal, oval, semicircular or even circular. The decisive factor is that, on all sides, they are accessed by and oriented toward the outside area. Even so, their basic geometric shape leads to different frameworks for architectural and urban design (e.g. sharp corners), the design and quality of the interior areas, and lighting conditions in apartments.

Blocks of buildings can be closed on all sides, or the edges can be interrupted and contain gaps. An open city block consists of short rows of terraced, semi-detached or single-family homes, but they must be situated so close to each other that they do not mar the impression of a block and appear to be solitaires. › Fig. 11

Designing
corners

A special challenge – and not only from an architectural perspective – lies in designing the corners of a block. For one thing, corners have a particularly favourable position (for shops, restaurants and other commercial facilities) because they can be accessed from both sides. For another, they are a critical point with a number of disadvantages: the rear (property) area is very small or there may be no rear space at all. Corners are unsuitable for private uses or expansion, and the narrow rear facade

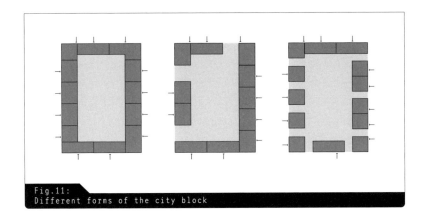

Fig.11:
Different forms of the city block

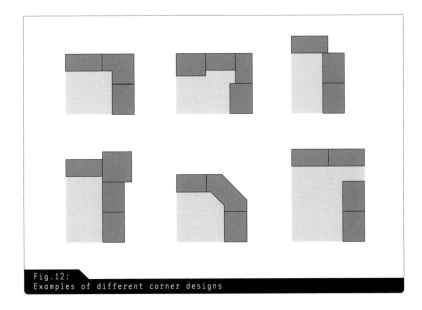

Fig.12:
Examples of different corner designs

may receive inadequate natural lighting, depending on the building's orientation.

The corners of city blocks can be designed with gaps so that the corner buildings receive adequate light. They can also be completely removed or "bevelled". Another possibility is to create especially wide or narrow corner buildings. › Fig. 12

21

FORMATION OF URBAN SPACE

Integration
into the city

The city block facilitates close integration into the surrounding urban structure. It is linked to the network of city streets and building lines, which define it spatially and geometrically. The city block is a continuous closed urban space, accessible from all sides, that ensures the continuity of surrounding structures and exterior urban areas.

The property's exterior boundary simultaneously defines the boundary between the public space of the city and the private space of the buildings and plot. As with the row, there are different ways to design this spatial transition, depending on whether the buildings stand directly on the street or are slightly recessed from it (e.g. through a front garden), on whether the ground floors serve residential or commercial purposes; and on whether the building has a basement floor. > Chapter The row

Front and rear

The different manner in which the front and rear sides are treated in designs reflects the clear spatial differentiation between the exterior (with its link to the public area of the city) and the interior (with its link to shared private space). This treatment covers not only the design of open space, but architectural design as well. The front facades with their link to the street, visible to everyone, are usually designed to meet a relatively high creative standard. Materials are selected which have an impressive, stately character, and the horizontal and vertical structure, the proportions and the architectural ornamentation of windows are subject to a high degree of creative discipline. By contrast, the rear, which is visible and accessible only to a limited degree to the general public and neighbours, is often designed to meet practical needs. Windows do not adhere to geometric organizational principles as rigidly, and their size and positions reflect the purposes for which they are used (kitchens, bathrooms, ancillary and sitting rooms). The architecture is more flexible and can be more easily adapted to changing requirements (such as extensions, remodelling

〗

\\ Note:
In 20th-century city blocks, which tend to have a more uniform design, the interior and exterior facades were often treated similarly due to a new conception of architecture and public space. The same is true of the otherwise different spatial characters of the inner and outer areas.

projects and conversions). All told, the city block is a spatial system that is extremely complex and flexible, and lends itself particularly well to integrating diverse, differentiated modes of behaviour, activities and forms of appropriation.

> 0

High density

By virtue of its rational and economic use of urban land, the city block allows a relatively high degree of urban density. This can be regarded as an important environmental and economic advantage given the current discussion of the increased use of land in the regions surrounding our cities.

FUNCTIONS, ORIENTATION AND ACCESS

Mixed uses

The city block is well suited to diverse functions and combined uses because of its direct integration into the broader spatial system, streets and squares of the city. Although the ground floors of buildings on a block are close to the street and lack privacy, they have proved an excellent location for shops, small businesses and restaurants over the centuries.

The flexible rear area of the city block can provide space for numerous activities and uses that find their architectural expression in supplementary buildings. In the Middle Ages and the *Gründerzeit*, there were often workshops inside blocks, and work and housing were closely intertwined. One also sees examples of entire factory buildings located inside a city block. > Fig. 13 Where required, the rear courtyards were accessed by entrance drives leading through the front buildings.

In the early 20th century, there was a move to banish the disruptive businesses from inside city blocks due to their noise and pollution. This occurred in connection with the Athens Charter, which recommended creating a clear separation between urban functions such as housing, work, recreation and transport. > Chapter The row Ever since, blocks have primarily been used for housing, and the internal area accommodates private and collective playgrounds, open spaces, gardens and planted areas.

It was not until the 1970s that balanced combinations of non-disruptive functions were once again introduced into the city. The transition from industrial to service society has changed workplaces, the possible disturbances they cause, and the ease with which they can be integrated into the surrounding residential area of a city quarter. In most cases, combined uses are not a problem, and indeed can create a special quality. The city block continues to offer excellent conditions for such combinations, even if not all blocks in a city or a neighbourhood have the same degree of density as regards commercial uses. This density is usually greatest

Fig.13:
Different ways that block interiors are used

〉✎

along main traffic routes, with nearby ground floors usually being used for residential purposes.

Building depth and orientation — Since the edges of a city block follow the course of the street, there are limitations on building orientation. In apartments oriented to both sides of the building, auxiliary rooms can be located in the interior area that is not illuminated by natural light (this is assuming that the average depth of east-west buildings is 11 to 13 m). Floor plans with a predominantly north-south orientation should be wider and have a shallower depth amounting to only about 9 to 11 m. This allows more effective use of the southern facade, which receives direct sunlight.

Aside from sunlight, other important factors for orienting apartments on a city block are street traffic and possible noise disturbances. In many cases, architects will have to weigh the benefits of orienting the apartment to the sun (despite the exposure to the street and street noise) against the benefits of orienting it to the quiet back courtyard, which may be on the shady side of the building. Here it is also advisable to have floor plans extend to both sides of the building in order to meet all needs.

Parking spaces are often arranged parallel, diagonal or perpendicular to the street in front of the city block. An attractive green cityscape can be created by breaking up this pattern through trees planted at regular intervals of about five to ten parking spaces. Due to the increased volume of traffic in modern cities, the available parking spaces will probably be insufficient to cover all needs. If this is the case, underground garages located under the buildings or the interior courtyard may be necessary to provide adequate parking. However, underground garages can place restrictions on the design of the open planted areas in the courtyard, and they can substantially increases costs. It is important not to place aboveground parking spaces inside the city block since this not only impairs the visual effect of the courtyard but also causes noise problems and conflicts with the otherwise quiet uses of the rear area.

HISTORICAL EXAMPLES

Ever since Antiquity, the city block has been one of the most important elements of urban design. It was used in Greek cities as early as the 6th century BC, and in the 5th century Hippodamus designed the newly founded city of Miletus on the basis of a regular orthogonal grid pattern. › Fig. 14 A large number of Greek colonies, including Olynthus, Agrigento, Paestum and Naples, were also laid out using the block system.

Roman town planning adopted the grid principle and applied it rigorously to its newly founded towns – Cologne, Trier, Nîmes, Bologna and Florence. These settlements usually evolved from a military camp, the *castrum*, and their backbone was formed by two main streets intersecting at right angles, the north-south *cardo maximus* and the east-west *decumanus maximus*. These axes divided the city into four areas › Fig. 15 giving us the term "city quarter". The market and important public buildings were

---

\\Tip:
To ensure a high degree of flexibility in the event of mixed uses, the height of a ground floor ceiling on a block can be slightly raised, particularly along main streets. A height of 3.0 or 3.25 m can replace the usual height of about 2.5 m required for residential purposes.

\\Tip:
As a rule of thumb, if the buildings on a block have a maximum of three storeys, it can be assumed that continuous diagonal parking along the street can meet parking requirements (one parking space per housing unit). However, if the buildings have more storeys, other solutions are required.

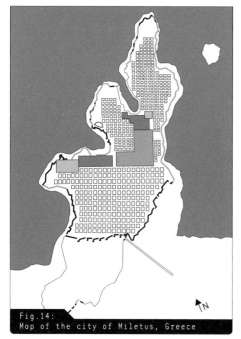

Fig.14:
Map of the city of Miletus, Greece

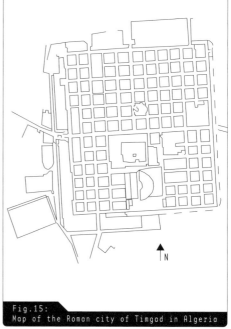

Fig.15:
Map of the Roman city of Timgad in Algeria

located at the intersection point of the main streets, and additional side streets were laid out parallel to them, creating block structures. Deviations from this grid pattern were caused by both special topographic characteristics of the cities (hills, rivers etc.) and the existing streets that were incorporated into the urban network. Difficult topographical locations could thus feature blocks shaped as triangles or different types of rectangles (polygons).

Medieval city blocks

In many places the layouts of Roman cities survived the massive decline in population and urban decay of the post-Roman period, before being revived in the Middle Ages. Although new buildings were erected on the Roman grid patterns, the street layout and block structure remained largely unchanged. Most of the new medieval towns and expanded urban areas that were not based on the Roman grid used a system of polygonal blocks of different shapes and sizes. This created a distinctive public urban space consisting of streets, paths and squares that provided access to the buildings and ensured social living and commerce. Contrasting with this were the private rear areas made up of auxiliary buildings, courtyards and gardens. › Fig. 16

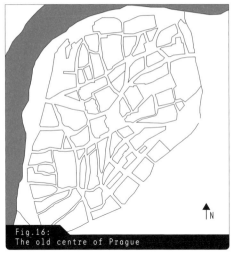

Fig.16:
The old centre of Prague

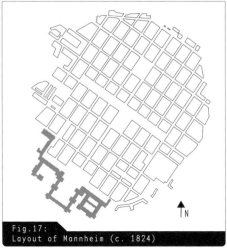

Fig.17:
Layout of Mannheim (c. 1824)

Cities in
colonies

The new cities of the Renaissance (such as the fortress town of Pal-manova, founded in 1593 northeast of Venice) and urban planning in the Baroque period (e.g. 17th-century Mannheim) adopted the model of regular grid patterns from Antiquity. › Fig. 17 The same is true of cities founded in North and South America. Spanish and Portuguese conquerors imported the idea of regularly laid out city blocks to the New World as a formal principle of urban design. These basic patterns have survived as central organizational structures to the present day in such cities as Mexico City, Lima, Caracas and Santo Domingo. One famous example in North America is Manhattan. Founded by Dutch immigrants, it uses a chessboard-like pattern as a basis for its urban layout. However, its current cityscape with high-rises and skyscrapers differs radically from traditional city blocks, where buildings are not as tall.

Cities in the
industrial age

The rapidly growing cities of the 19th-century industrial age adopted the block structure because of its many advantages: integration into the city as a whole, highly diverse uses, and high level of structural and popu-lation density.

During the expansion of Berlin in the German *Gründerzeit* (1871–1914), town planners went so far as to build densely developed blocks with multiple rear courtyards that were accessed from the street through en-trance drives. This combination of a very small section of street with a deep plot and high building density facilitated better utilization of the

27

Fig.18:
Gründerzeit block structures in Prenzlauer Berg, Berlin

available land. However, due to these dense developments, many rooms in the rear courtyard apartments – which housed up to 15 people – did not receive direct sunlight or even sufficient daylight. Because of the population density of far more than 1,000 people per hectare, the hygienic conditions were totally inadequate in most cases, and the living conditions were catastrophic. Tuberculosis and other epidemics were widespread. › Fig. 18

As early as the 19th century, these poor social and hygienic conditions were sharply criticized by many, including Friedrich Engels in his 1845 work *The Condition of the Working Class in England*. In the early 20th century, this criticism led to a partial reform of the city block. In "modern" blocks, planted areas replaced the buildings once erected in the rear courtyards, as illustrated by the projects of Hendrik Petrus Berlage in Amsterdam, J.J.P. Oud in Rotterdam, and Fritz Schumacher in Hamburg.

In the 1920s, the exponents of *Neues Bauen* › Chapter The row fought to have the closed blocks replaced by the freestanding ribbon as a major structural element of the city. › Chapter The ribbon This development fundamentally changed the appearance of European cities. For several decades afterward, the city block became considerably less important as an urban element.

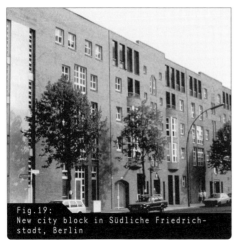

Fig.19:
New city block in Südliche Friedrichstadt, Berlin

Fig.20:
Quiet communal areas inside the blocks
in Südliche Friedrichstadt

The renaissance
of the city
block

> 🖼

It was not until the 1960s and then the 1970s and 1980s that the city block made a comeback in France, Italy, Germany and other European countries. The catalyst was the criticism many levelled at the destructive effects that modern architecture and *Neues Bauen* had had on cities. The projects built for the International Building Exhibition in Berlin (IBA) between 1980 and 1990 were an expression of this changed philosophy, which also went under the heading of "city repair." > Figs. 19 and 20

Today the city block is once again an important tool in the urban planning repertoire, and even the *Gründerzeit* neighbourhoods that were

🖼
\\Note:
In 1966, the architect and theoretician Aldo
Rossi published an influential book entitled
L'architettura della città (English edition:
The Architecture of the City). In this work
Rossi emphasizes the role block structures play
in creating urban space. He also stresses the
continuity (permanence) of such structures and
their importance for societies, social identity
and history.

29

criticized just a few years back are enjoying great popularity due to their urban density and mixed uses. Rear courtyards are no longer being cleared of all buildings, even if they are packed very close together. Rather, owners are often converting these buildings into attractive and unusual forms of housing and putting them to other uses (studios, lofts, non-disruptive small business). New structures are even being built inside blocks where there is sufficient space.

\\ Note:
The dense block structures of 19th-century industrial cities have gained a new appeal because population density has declined substantially while development density has remained the same. Nowadays it is not uncommon for two people to live in a three-room apartment that a century ago may have housed 25 to 30 individuals.

THE COURTYARD (INVERSE BLOCK)

In terms of urban organization, the courtyard can be seen as the inversion of the city block. The formal arrangement of buildings can be identical for the block and the courtyard, but while buildings on the block (i.e. those along the edge of the block) are accessed from the outside, the buildings of a courtyard are accessed from the inside. Consequently, the front sides of the courtyard buildings are oriented toward the inside space and the rear sides to the outside. The interior area becomes – at least partially – a public space.

> ⋂

As used in urban planning terminology, the term "courtyard" derives from typological models such as the enclosed farmyard or monastery complexes in which the buildings are grouped in cloisters around a courtyard. The term therefore refers to an ensemble of buildings with an open area that is central to its formal and functional organization. As a whole, these architectural ensembles have a self-contained, introverted character.

FORM AND SPATIAL STRUCTURE

Courtyards are usually designed as a complete unit. Their layout is largely based on the principle of neighbourly and collective existence.
> Fig. 21

Outer
boundaries

Courtyards can be enclosed by very similar buildings, or they can consist of a group of buildings with different formal designs. In both cases an important feature is that the edges of the courtyard are largely closed off spatially. Aside from entranceways and entrance drives, no large gaps should remain that disrupt the detached quality of the courtyard. If the

⋂
\\ Note:
The word *close* is also used in English-
speaking countries. It originates from
claustrum, the Latin word for cloisters
(monastery), which means "closed off." The
German word *Klause* can be used in this context
as well (a building or group of buildings
closed off from the outside; a hermitage).

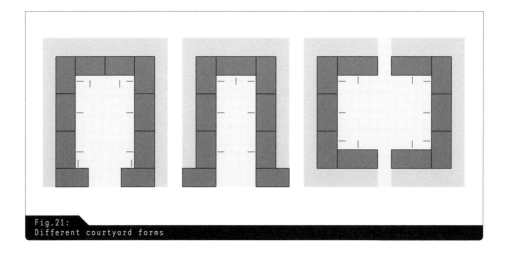

Fig.21:
Different courtyard forms

buildings themselves do not form boundaries, they may be created by other "edge-making" elements, such as walls and hedges.

Like the city block, the courtyard can have entirely different geometric forms. As a forecourt or entrance court, for instance, it can also function as a sub-element in a block structure.

Since the front sides of courtyard buildings face inwards and the exterior sides overlook public space (provided the courtyard is not entirely surrounded by other buildings), the facades on both sides must fulfil specific design requirements. In contrast to the city block, the high degree of formal and creative control required for the courtyard interior does not permit a great deal of freedom for random, unplanned or unauthorized installations and extensions. In a courtyard, there is little distinction between front and back – or outside and inside – in the design of facades and the use of materials.

FORMATION OF URBAN SPACE

Semi-open spaces

The courtyard is detached from the integrated system of public streets and access routes. While it is usually accessible to the public (or else the buildings could not be entered), it constitutes a space with a limited public character that can best be described as semi-public. The design of the transitions between urban space and the courtyard are particularly important and can make use of spatial constrictions, height differences

32

created by ramps and stairs, as well as entrance drives. Architects can also incorporate different ground coverings, planting and other features.

Courtyards are not intertwined as tightly with the urban environment as city blocks, and they are less suited for urban integration. › Chapter The city block The entrances are often pathways that terminate in dead ends and that deliberately do not continue the urban network due to the desire for introversion. The courtyard remains a small world in and of itself. Using a spatial sequence of courtyards that ultimately lead to public street space, this urban element can be better integrated into its environment. The courtyard then becomes a kind of arcade. › Chapter The arcade

FUNCTIONS, ORIENTATION AND ACCESS

Collective use   The courtyard often serves as an urban design model for collective (or cooperative) housing. It offers residents a point of reference and a centre for creating spaces with a degree of privacy and tranquillity, removed from the hustle and bustle of the surrounding city. The courtyard forms a partially autonomous unit within a neighbourhood. This can enhance the residents' sense of security and their ability to monitor the collective space, since the people who live and work in a courtyard will know each other and immediately notice strangers. By orienting important elements toward the outside (such as access routes, open areas and even common spaces), architects can accentuate the courtyard's claim to being a social space. Combined uses are also possible. Special functions and non-disruptive service businesses such as offices and medical practices can be integrated into this urban element.

The courtyard faces similar orientation and lighting problems to the city block. And here, too, many variations have been used in the design of corner areas. › Chapter The city block The inner corner is a special challenge since the rather small front of the building facing the courtyard corresponds to a large exterior area on the garden or rear side.

High degree   The courtyard allows urban land to be optimally exploited for archi-
of development   tectural purposes. In combination with the city block, it is often used to
density   enhance building density. Since it is entered from the inside, it can provide access to additional land in the very rear of the plot.

Beyond its access-providing function, the inner space of a courtyard can be a place of shared exchanges, a playground for children, a meeting spot, a storage space for bicycles and prams, a delivery zone, a shared park and recreation area, and much more. If possible, parking spaces for cars should not be located in this inner space to avoid undermining its recreational quality and residential tranquillity. They should be placed outside courtyards or in an underground garage beneath them. › Chapter The city block

HISTORICAL EXAMPLES

Courtyard
houses

Houses structured around one or more courtyards were first built in the ancient world and can still be found today, particularly in the Mediterranean region. Such structures were especially widespread in Islamic architecture. However, from an urban planning perspective, this type of courtyard house must be seen as a borderline example of the courtyard as urban building block since it is usually constructed on a single piece of land.

Farmhouses and
monasteries

As additional historical examples, we can point to the farmhouse and monastery complexes found in many regions that are for the most part closed off spatially to the outside. What both monasteries and farmhouses have in common is that they are not built solely for residential purpose. The protection they provide from the outside and the shielded social space they create within are important aspects of each. The Certosa in Pavia in northern Italy, an extension of a monastery that provides housing for monks, has a close resemblance to a courtyard structure. › Fig. 22

Charitable
housing
projects

The residential complexes that Jakob Fugger built for the poor in Augsburg in the period around 1520 can be regarded as an example of communal courtyards from early modern times. They are based on the *hofjes* that were built in the Middle Ages, particularly in Dutch cities. These

\\Tip:
If an underground car park is required, it can make sense to raise the height of the courtyard by about 1 m in relation to the surrounding area. This will shorten the length of the car park's entrance ramp and permit natural ventilation through the exterior walls.

\\Note:
The *Wiener Gemeindebauten* in "Red Vienna" was the Social Democratic government's response to the housing shortage among the working population. As part of an extensive construction program launched in 1923, it set out to build up to 30,000 apartments annually. The *Wiener Höfe* (Viennese courtyards) emerged — monumental housing projects with high ceilings, shared courtyards and many subsequent housing facilities. The best known is the Karl-Marx-Hof, which contains more than 1,300 housing units, numerous businesses and communal facilities.

Fig.22:
Courtyard in Certosa di Pavia

charitable facilities, which date as far back as the 13th century, were often set up as foundations that provided housing for needy groups in society, including elderly people, the poor, the sick and orphans. One of the best-known examples is the Begijnhof in Amsterdam.

Social movements have repeatedly taken up the courtyard concept since it guarantees a minimum amount of shared open space and also offers a degree of privacy despite its high density. Nineteenth-century industrialists used this urban building block as a paternalistic housing model for their workers for the same reason. Even the sprawling "Wiener Gemeindebauten" (Viennese communal housing blocks) built in the 1920s were based on the courtyard; and Michiel Brinkman made use of a similar concept when designing the large city courtyard in Rotterdam-Spangen that accommodated some 270 families (built between 1919 and 1922). Apart from entrances on the ground floor, a wraparound outdoor corridor on the second floor provided access to the apartments. › Fig. 23

> ⑩

Courtyards in
the garden city

In the early 20th century, courtyards surrounded by terraced houses were used by the garden city movement as an architectural model for quiet,

35

Fig.23:
Residential courtyard with outdoor
corridors in Rotterdam-Spangen, designed by Michiel Brinkman (1919–1922)

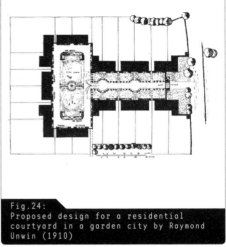

Fig.24:
Proposed design for a residential
courtyard in a garden city by Raymond
Unwin (1910)

group-based housing on planted grounds. Here, the courtyards were called
"closes". Neighbourhood familiarity and small-town identity played a special role. The architect Raymond Unwin designed attractive examples of
"closes" in the garden cities of Letchworth, Welwyn Garden City and Hamp-
stead Garden Suburb in the south of England. > Fig. 24

> 🛈

Courtyards continue to be used in the design of communal housing
projects, particularly in experimental or cooperative housing construction.

🛈
\\ Note:
In his work *Town Planning in Practice*, which
was first published in 1910, Raymond Unwin
describes the functional characteristics and
design features of residential courtyards in
new housing estates. He also refers to their
economical use of the site and the broad vista
that residents in the surrounding buildings
have of the planted square and open areas.

THE ARCADE

The arcade has generally evolved as a roofed-over street, lined with shops and businesses, that leads between lines of buildings from one place to the next. The arcade is structurally related to the courtyard in that it is accessed from the inside.

FORM AND SPATIAL STRUCTURE

Glass-covered
streets

In most cases, the arcade is a shopping and commercial street covered by a glass roof. As a public path, it is usually accessible only to pedestrians. It is enclosed on both sides by the facades of the adjoining buildings, which are usually carefully designed to create a prestigious impression. Merchandise displayed in the shops on the street is visible to all from behind large windows.

Arcades can be straight, angular or curved. They can take almost any possible linear form or branch off in different directions. The broader spaces at these intersection points can create small squares where people can linger. › Fig. 25

Arcades may run between two different buildings (and sometimes even have several floors). They may also take the form of public paths running through compact block structures. Where this is the case, a great deal of attention is usually paid to the design of the inside facades. In such cases the interior facades are usually carefully designed to reflect the formal characteristics of the exterior.

Fig. 25:
Different arcade forms

Fig.26:
Galleria Vittorio Emanuele II in Milan

FORMATION OF URBAN SPACE

Network of paths
The arcade connects paths in the city. This is especially true of the well-known 19th-century arcades in Paris, Brussels, London, Naples and Milan. For instance, the famous Galleria Vittorio Emanuele II in Milan is the shortest route between two important city sites – the cathedral and La Scala opera house. › Fig. 26 Sometimes arcades can create shortcuts that optimize the access network of the city, at least for pedestrians. The glass-roofed arcades in Hamburg, which offer protection from the weather, still provide an important secondary access system to the centre of town.

Climate buffer
As a result of the arcade's roof, a climate buffer emerges inside that considerably enhances the arcade's appeal as a place to tarry, particularly during the inclement seasons of the year. Nowadays a large number of arcades are heated in winter and air-conditioned in summer – but this requires clear spatial separations. Where these exist, the arcade assumes the character of an interior space much like a department store and is separated from the urban space of the city, although this detracts from its image as a continuous covered street space.

Fig.27:
New arcade in the centre of Aveiro, Portugal

FUNCTIONS, ORIENTATION AND ACCESS

Arcades are primarily influenced by "economic" considerations since in prime inner city locations they can also provide accessibility to the interior plots on a block. Their walkways are largely flat and level so as not to disturb strollers or divert their attention from exhibits and displays in shop windows. › Fig. 27

Commercial uses   Retail and commercial uses predominate and are in some cases supplemented by restaurants. Housing is an exception, but if apartments are included in the arcade, the roof glazing generally begins below the apartments in order to protect against fire, or for lighting and ventilation. Thus it can be said that housing only influences the space of an arcade if the building and apartment entrances are located in the interior.

A key factor, not only for the arcade's commercial success, is functional integration into the urban environment. Both the front and rear of the arcade are important. Architects must make sure that the various entrances lie on lively, busy streets, for if this is not the case, it will cause

Fig.28:
Hustle and bustle in the Cairo bazaar

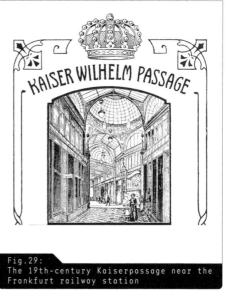

Fig.29:
The 19th-century Kaiserpassage near the
Frankfurt railway station

an imbalance between an attractive front area and a less attractive rear area.

HISTORICAL EXAMPLES

Forums and
bazaars

Ancient Rome had spatial structures that can be seen as the forerunners of arcades. The Forum Iulium and the Trajan's Market were both lined by shops and businesses, and the street between them was a place for people to linger and conduct business. The Persian city of Isfahan also has a very similar spatial structure. The bazaars and souks in the Islamic world continue to use this organizational principle to the present day. Booths are rowed together on both sides of a central path for the display of various goods. › Fig. 28

Arcades in the
19th century

Arcades became fashionable in European cities such as Paris, Milan and Vienna in the 19th century. They provided the affluent middle classes with a place to stroll that was protected from the weather – and a space that was removed from the noise and dirt of the street. › Fig. 29 The arcades served the economic interests of vendors by making entertainment and pleasure the focus of their design, organization and presentational techniques. Yet they also had a representational function for the wealthy middle classes and the city itself.

› 🛈

40

> 🔖

The model of the arcade as a locus of commerce and presentation can be seen as informing the development of present-day shopping centres and large shopping malls. But in contrast to their historical predecessor, these structures are not integrated into the surrounding city. From the outside, they are uninspiring, nondescript "boxes" that usually negate the characteristics necessary to create urban space. > Chapter The shed

🔖

\\ Note:
The most important work on arcades is *Passagen-Werk* by Walter Benjamin (English edition: *The Arcades Project*). It consists of literary and architectural reflections on the arcades of the 19th century. The diverse commentary creates a broad impression of the aesthetic design and the economic and functional importance of arcades as social arenas and places of commerce. Benjamin also addresses the physical aspect of walking, describing the arcades as places where strollers observed the displayed goods and services partially out of "scientific" interest and partially for amusement.

🔖

\\ Note:
In the book *Project on the City: Harvard Design School Guide to Shopping*, published in 2001, a group of writers under the architect and theoretician Rem Koolhaas associatively examine the historical development of shopping streets and centres, juxtaposing a series of images of Roman fora and Persian and Arab bazaars with today's shopping centres and malls.

THE RIBBON

Ribbons (*Zeilen*) are linear, freestanding urban elements that are deliberately oriented away from the street space to achieve "hygienic" advantages such as the best possible exposure to light and ventilation. They were developed in the 1920s as a reaction to the overcrowded urban space created by the block structures and corridor streets of the traditional city. They can thus be understood as a critique of living conditions in the tenements constructed in the late 19th century. › Chapter The city block

FORM AND SPATIAL STRUCTURE

The ribbon can be seen as a further development of the row. However, in contrast, it is not designed to form a bordered street space. In most cases only its "head," or short side, is oriented toward the access street. This independence from the street vector allows the ribbon to be oriented to achieve maximum exposure to sunlight.

Ribbons are thus not parallel but perpendicular to the street and are accessed via a secondary footpath (in some cases a cul-de-sac). › Fig. 30 Access to ribbon developments is usually from the side less favoured by the sun, i.e. the east or north side (in the southern hemisphere, the south

Fig.30:
Additive ribbon development

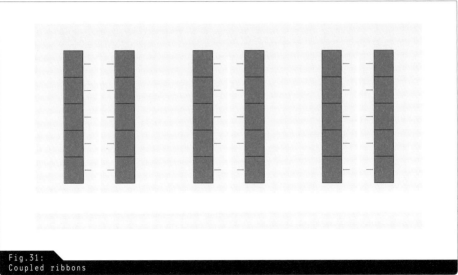

Fig.31:
Coupled ribbons

side). This prevents access paths from disturbing the sunnier southern and western sides. These sides are commonly used for private open spaces such as balconies, loggias, roof terraces and, on the ground floors, small garden plots.

Additive
ribbons

The additive repetition of this pattern in ribbon developments creates an extensive urban structure in which the front side of each ribbon faces the back of the adjacent one. This direct juxtaposition of rear (private) and front (public) spaces can result in a lack of spatial clarity, although this conflict can be mitigated by delimiting ribbons from one another using vegetation, varying structural levels and outbuildings such as bicycle and storage sheds.

Coupled ribbons

Another possibility consists in a mirrored rather than an additive arrangement of ribbons and their access paths. The result is a series of "coupled" ribbons with the open spaces between the ribbons containing either adjacent front areas or adjacent rear areas in an alternating pattern. › Fig. 31 This arrangement means that apartments and in particular their adjoining open spaces have different orientations to the sun, but it has the advantage of lending the external space a social character.

Ribbons can be composed of single-family houses joined in a line (in the form of terraced houses of between two and three storeys) or joined multiple-family dwellings (connected apartment blocks of between three and six storeys). The slab structure used for large unitary residential complexes with eight or more storeys is often referred to as a special form of the ribbon development.

Most ribbon structures are linear, but they can also be curved, angled or consist of a number of sections set off from one another. Along with differences in length and height, such variations can provide a rudimentary tool for shaping urban space.

Standardization The ribbon can be understood as typical of the age of mass production. Its linearity and the repetition of individual units make it highly amenable to the use of industrially prefabricated elements. However, the capacity for standardization that this allows (which makes for a highly economical building process) can mean a risk – in the case of persistent repetition – of monotonous forms and urban designs. An example is the industrially prefabricated high-rise apartment blocks built on many large-scale housing estates in the second half of the 20th century, which are found above all in Eastern Europe.

FORMATION OF URBAN SPACE

The orientation of ribbons toward light and the sun results in their almost complete independence from the surrounding urban space and the local network of access streets. In this sense the ribbon negates traditional concepts of urban form and space. This independence often results in it becoming an anti-urban element that makes no claim to a spatially formative role in the conventional sense. This is particularly problematic when ribbon developments – which originated as structural components of city peripheries – are built on inner-city wasteland and in the gaps between buildings.

Flowing space In cases where the areas between ribbons are not enclosed, the result is usually a flowing surrounding space that lacks clearly defined public and private areas. Usually covered by a lawn or other vegetation, this homogeneous space is in principle supposed to function as a communal area, particularly where the ribbon structure is made up of apartment blocks. However, such communal areas are rarely utilized in practice. Instead they remain anonymous spaces for which no one feels responsible and they quickly fall into neglect. › Fig. 32 Furthermore, due to the lack of defined street space, these open areas are subject to only a low level of social control, which can contribute to residents' feelings of insecurity, particularly in the case of large apartment blocks.

Fig.32:
Neglected spaces between the ribbon
structures of a modern housing estate

Fig.33:
Low transverse buildings that can be
used for commercial purposes close off
the space between ribbons from the
street.

FUNCTIONS, ORIENTATION AND ACCESS

Residential use As an urban building block, the ribbon accords with the concepts of functionalist urban design, which – as seen in the Athens Charter (1933) – strictly separates housing, work, transport and recreational functions. › Chapter The row For this reason ribbons are generally only used for residential buildings, with office and commercial uses being the exception. Due to its deviation from the access street and thus the lack of a direct view of the building from passing traffic, the ribbon does not readily lend itself to such public uses.

This is also the reason that small shops and other providers of daily services are sometimes located in the short front section of the ribbon, directly on the access street or in low intermediary buildings between the ribbons. › Fig. 33 These structures have a dual urban-planning function. They restore a degree of continuity to the public street space, and they also shield the areas between the ribbons both spatially and acoustically from the street. As a result the urban space on both sides becomes more clearly defined – a first step back toward shaping urban space. A mixed form is produced that combines the ribbon with the (open) block and includes quiet, semi-public spaces.

Orientation As in rows and blocks, apartments in ribbon developments can be differentiated into those with an east-west orientation and those with a north-south orientation. An east-west orientation has the advantage that recreational rooms receive sunlight from both sides, whereas a north-south orientation provides natural light from only one side. For this reason, orientation is an important factor when considering building depth and how open floor plans should be. > Chapters The row, The city block

Residential pathways

Since ribbons are connected to the street network only on their short sides, building entrances are usually accessed via footpaths along one side. However, in some cases we find an alternating pattern of roadways and footpaths such that a ribbon can be accessed on one side via a cul-de-sac and on the other via a footpath. This in turn has an effect on the internal organization of ribbon developments in terms of the location of main entrances and individual rooms within the apartments and the orientation of open areas. The advantage of this pattern is that it allows for a separation between motorized and non-motorized traffic. The footpaths leading to the ribbons often take on a semi-public character, which, outside entrance doors, promotes recreation and communication, say, between playing children.

Outside areas

For a long time ground-floor residents – whose apartments tend to be slightly elevated above ground level – were not permitted to use any outside areas directly in front of their apartments. Appropriating the green areas in front of apartments was regarded as contrary to the principle of "equal rights for all". Only recently has it been recognized that residents do not necessarily share the same interests in this regard. Some would like a small garden while others prefer a balcony or roof terrace. Furthermore, allowing ground-floor residents to have a small garden or terrace area leads to an improvement in the aesthetic quality of outside spaces, a greater feeling of responsibility for their care, and better social supervision. This benefits the general security of the whole residential community.

HISTORICAL EXAMPLES

The ribbon is a comparatively new urban building block. With the exception of a few historical forerunners, such as the Adelphi development in London, which was built between 1768 and 1772 by the brothers James und Robert Adam, or the blocks with outdoor-corridor access that were built in northern Italy in the late 19th century, the ribbon development was essentially a creation of the *Neues Bauen* movement of the 1920s.

Residential estates in the 1920s

The most prominent example is the Dammerstock residential estate, which was built in 1927–1928 in Karlsruhe as an exhibition project. > Fig. 34 The final version of the site plan was designed by Otto Haesler and Walter Gropius, who was director of the Bauhaus at the time. The plan was a deliberately provocative manifesto for a completely new type of urban structure. It proposed a strict north-south ribbon vector with an east-

Fig.34:
Site plan of the Dammerstock housing estate, showing a rigid ribbon structure adhering strictly to a north-south vector

west orientation for all apartments, a seemingly endless linearity, identical intervals between the individual ribbons and the abandonment of all conventional notions of spatial organization. There is probably no other urban-planning project that has created such a degree of controversy from its inception. While some saw the estate as an embodiment of modern, progressive urban development, providing optimal living conditions (light, air, sun) for everyone, others denounced its stubborn adherence to the principles that informed the abstract estate ground plan, the uniform architecture and lack of spatial formation. › Fig. 35

\\ Note:
Blocks with outdoor-corridor access are elongated ribbon developments containing connected residential units. They are accessed on one or more levels by a shared outside walkway.

\\ Note:
The representatives of modern architecture focused on the ribbon primarily because of the progress it made in urban "hygiene" and because of the social implications it had for life in an egalitarian society that offered the same residential and living conditions for all. They also emphasized the economic advantages this urban element offered for the mass production of building elements. The theory of ribbon development was systematically and comprehensively discussed and documented for the first time within the context of the "Rational Site Planning" segment of the CIAM congress held in Brussels in 1930.

Fig.35:
Stringently organized ribbon development in the Dammerstock housing estate in Karlsruhe

The model established by the Dammerstock residential estate inspired numerous other well-known *Neues Bauen* projects in the late 1920s, such as the Hellerhof estate (1929–1932) and the Westhausen estate (1929–1931) in Frankfurt, Siemensstadt (1929–1932) and Haselhorst (1928–1931) in Berlin, and the Rothenburg estate in Kassel (1929–1931). In the 1950s and 1960s, this urban-planning concept was taken up across Europe and in other parts of the world as the blueprint for a standardized form of residential building for lower-income earners.

Modernization programmes

In the 1970s, the ribbon development as an urban component became the target of the postmodern critique of functionalist architecture in general. It fell into disrepute primarily because of the social problems engendered by the predominance of economically disadvantaged residents, its functional inadequacy as a so-called dormitory town and its aesthetic monotony. However, since the 1990s, modernization programmes and design improvements (the addition of generous balcony spaces, demolition of buildings that are too high, remodelling of the surrounding environment) have succeeded in improving residential conditions in many ribbon development neighbourhoods.

THE SOLITAIRE

In urban-planning terms, a solitaire refers to a building that either stands alone or is clearly distinguishable from its urban surroundings. Freestanding buildings such as granges, farmhouses, castles and monasteries have been part of the cultural landscape since time immemorial. However, in the more densely built context of the city, solitaires initially tended to be defined by the fact that they protruded from the regular network of urban elements constituted by rows and blocks. They were usually public buildings (temples, churches, town halls) or the buildings of the ruling classes (castles, fortresses). They were later built as residences for the rich (villas, palaces) or to house the growing urban infrastructure (schools, theatres, opera houses, museums, hospitals, parliament buildings, universities etc.). Today, the solitaires found in large cities include residential and office towers as well as freestanding, single-family homes that use up an increasing amount of land.

FORM AND SPATIAL STRUCTURE

Solitaires are quite distinctive from the surrounding buildings in terms of their size, importance, geometry, architectural design and construction materials. In cases where they are not spatially separated from neighbouring structures, their distinctiveness in terms of form and decoration make them clearly recognizable as self-defined structural units.
› Fig. 36

Formal
autonomy

Where a solitaire is not connected with any other buildings, its design can be relatively independent from the urban-planning context in terms of form and proportions. This means that architects have far more creative latitude than when designing other urban building blocks, with the result that solitaires can take the form of slabs, towers, cubes, cylinders, pyramids, and a range of hybrid combinations. Nevertheless, if they need to be integrated into a larger urban ensemble or have a specific relevance for the urban silhouette or the landscape, the size, form and facades of solitaires should accord with certain design principles.

FORMATION OF URBAN SPACE

The design concept for a solitaire does not seek to establish any direct connection with the buildings around it. In many cases, the aim is to create a structure that is obviously distinct from its urban framework and creates a particular focus in the cityscape and a specific spatial effect.

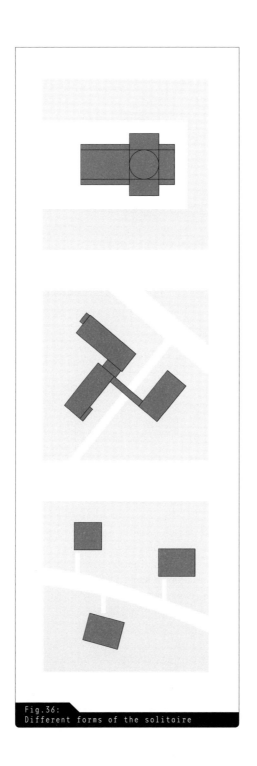

Fig.36:
Different forms of the solitaire

Fig.37:
The Temple Mount in Dougga, a town in Tunisia occupied by the ancient Romans

In some cases, solitaires are deliberately disconnected from the urban framework and placed in a prominent location. Examples of this can be seen in the temples and shrines of Antiquity. Such buildings do not specifically shape the urban space. Rather, they form vivid, sculptural culminations of an overall urban context, which they accentuate and orchestrate. Placing the structure in a topographically prominent location can strengthen this effect, as illustrated by the Acropolis in Athens and many other church and religious buildings. › Fig. 37 In the Baroque and absolutist periods, and later in 19th-century cities, town planners gave solitaires particular emphasis by building them at the ends or intersections of important thoroughfares and visual axes. › Fig. 38

However, the lack of space in densely built cities often means that solitaires do not stand completely alone. They are often spatially integrated into the side of a city square, a building line or a building group. › Fig. 39 This is particularly evident in dense, compact medieval cities, where large cathedrals, town halls, convents and even tithe barns are integrated into

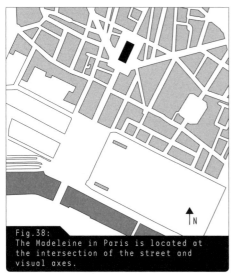

Fig.38:
The Madeleine in Paris is located at the intersection of the street and visual axes.

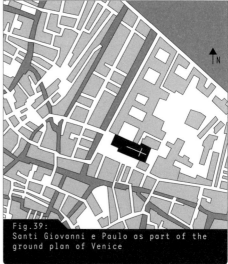

Fig.39:
Santi Giovanni e Paulo as part of the ground plan of Venice

the urban framework while remaining distinct from their surroundings due to their size, facade design and particular position within the city layout.

Spatial effect

In the cities of modernity, solitaires were usually built as completely freestanding buildings whose orientation allowed optimal lighting and ventilation. › Chapter The ribbon This was also a result of changed concepts of urban space, which, according to the objectives of the *Neues Bauen* movement, needed to be open and flowing rather than closed in the traditional manner. In this type of an urban space, which is characterized above all by the interplay between freely placed individual buildings, solitaires can have a pronounced spatial-sculptural effect. › Fig. 40

FUNCTIONS, ORIENTATION AND ACCESS

Functional specialization

In principle the solitaire can take on a range of functions as an urban building block. Although in the case of large buildings mixed uses are possible (e.g. commercial uses on the ground floors of residential high rises), the solitaire is usually characterized by a high degree of functional specialization, which encompasses specific public functions (town hall, community centre, school, university, museum etc.) and private uses that the design seeks to accommodate through a specific architectural identity (residential complex, government authority, business headquarters, hotel).

Fig.40:
Le Corbusier's Unité d'habitation in
Marseilles: a solitaire serving as a
prototype of the "vertical city"

Orientation

Orientation and natural lighting generally do not present problems for solitaires. If they are not unusually deep or wide buildings, which can result in dark areas in the interior, solitaires receive sunlight and can be ventilated from all sides. Problems with shadows can occur where high-rise blocks are built too closely together. This can be seen in some inner-city locations such as New York and in the mega-cities of East and Southeast Asia, including Beijing, Shanghai, Hong Kong and Seoul.

Car parks

The open areas usually found in front of, beside or behind the building generally make it possible to locate car parks at ground level. However,

\\ Note:
Le Corbusier's "machines for living"
– particularly the Unité d'habitation, which
was constructed in Marseilles between 1945 and
1952 for 1,300 residents – are examples of
the attempt to create "vertical cities" that
provide living space in green surroundings
for a broad range of income groups. In his
essay collection La Ville Radieuse, published
in 1935, Le Corbusier describes multi-storey
buildings that appear to float on pylons

above the ground, and that make nature an
integral element of the living space. These
solitaire residential buildings were envisaged
as completely independent of their urban
surroundings. As a consequence, their internal
structure is complex and includes not only
apartments but also shopping streets, communal
spaces, a hotel, kindergartens, roof terraces and
sporting facilities.

this may conflict with other proposed uses for the surrounding space (recreation, social interaction). For this reason, underground car parks are preferable, particularly in high-density residential and public buildings, which may require a large amount of parking at particular times.

HISTORICAL EXAMPLES

Reference has already been made to the individual, freestanding house as a basic building block of settlement structures, primarily in rural and village contexts, as well as to the solitaires associated with religious or secular authorities in ancient and medieval cities.

Palaces and villas

From the 15th century onwards, the palaces of important city residents took on increasing significance as solitaires within the urban landscape. A great deal of money was spent on structures that adequately represented the power of influential families, as can be seen in the Palazzo Pitti and the Palazzo Strozzi in Florence and the Fuggerhaus in Augsburg. However, in the age of absolutism, the significance attached to these patrician buildings shifted to the palaces of the nobility and the seats of royalty. Their sheer size clearly distinguished them from the houses of the urban bourgeoisie with their relatively small structural elements and often Gothic character. In the 16th century, Andrea Palladio created a form of villa architecture in Italy's Veneto region that became internationally renowned for its proportionality, formal expression and charm. It continues to serve as a paradigm today. > Fig. 41

Urban infrastructures

The expanding industrial city of the 19th century produced an array of new functional requirements as regards commercial, cultural, social, political and transport infrastructure. The prestigious solitaires – market halls, department stores, theatres, opera houses, museums, educational institutions, hospitals, parliament buildings, railway stations and many

\\ Note:
In his famous *Four Books on Architecture* (1570), a standard work on architectural theory, Palladio describes his villa buildings as examples of rural architecture, yet he does not position them as antithetical to the city.

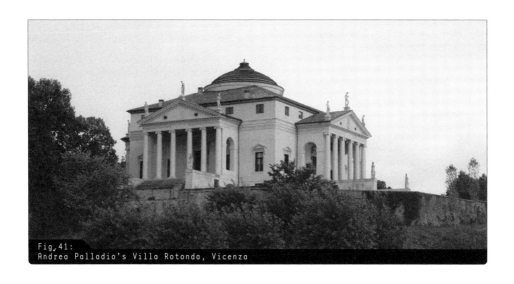

Fig. 41:
Andrea Palladio's Villa Rotonda, Vicenza

other types of public buildings – now assumed a high level of urban-planning significance and became a dominant element in urban space.

The car as individual transport in 20th-century cities contributed to a further quantitative and qualitative leap in urban development. The new level of mobility the car provided led to the extensive construction of solitaires in the form of freestanding single-family homes on the edges of cities and towns, above all in the prosperous countries of the industrialized world. They in turn resulted in the progressive depletion of open space and the destruction of rural landscapes. › Fig. 42 Furthermore, this development generated significant costs for infrastructure such as roads and sewage systems, and meant that a significant proportion of the population had to travel a long way to reach social, cultural and commercial facilities.

By contrast, in the field of high-rise construction, the solitaire allows for greater density. Even so, at least in the case of apartment complexes, the structural density is not greater than that found in rows and blocks of four to six levels because of the space that must be left between buildings. Furthermore, many residential solitaires tend to lack an urban-planning context, meaning they do not create urban spaces that correspond to the human need for orientation and security. › Fig. 43 When designing high-rise residential buildings, it is therefore necessary not only to select an appropriate location but also to define the intended target groups precisely. While this residential form is unsuitable for families with children, older people and socially disadvantaged groups, it can provide an attractive and

Fig.42:
Expansive freestanding single-family
houses in a suburban estate

Fig.43:
Vertical density in a freestanding
high-rise complex

exclusive alternative for young professionals, couples, single people and
more affluent sections of the population.

City villas The city villas constructed in recent decades are solitary residential
buildings between four and six storeys tall. In urban-planning terms, they
are an intermediate form between the single-family house and the high-
rise residential building.

Skyscrapers The skyscraper is a special form of the solitaire. Examples such as
bank towers and company headquarters are deliberately designed as spec-
tacular buildings that project a powerful corporate image. However, their
effect from a distance is quite different from the one they have close-up.
From a distance, skyscrapers can be fascinating, needle-like structures
reaching to the sky. They can even form groups, › Chapter The group with a
decisive influence on the silhouette of the city, as seen by the skylines
of Frankfurt › Fig. 44 and – even more impressively – New York. However,
from the perspective of the pedestrian or motorist the same buildings are
experienced less as solitaires than as objects that define the street space.
For this reason the design of their facades and the relationship between
the interior and exterior of the lower levels is extremely important. If
possible, these levels should have functions that allow public access in
order to inject life into the street spaces of otherwise mono-functional
› 🗋 office districts.

Fig.44:
The Frankfurt skyline

"Trans-
locational"
solitaires

In recent times, the comprehensive mediatization and globalization of our societies has produced a building type that could be described as a "translocational" solitaire. One example is the Frank Gehry's Guggenheim Museum in Bilbao, with which many people are familiar although they themselves have never visited it. › Fig. 45 This museum has become so engrained in the general consciousness that it constitutes a kind of virtual architecture that exerts an influence without being physically present. An analogous effect was no doubt created in earlier periods by structures such

\\ Note:
The 1960s saw renewed discussion of the relevance of striking solitaires for urban design. In his book *The Image of the City*, Kevin Lynch points to the great significance of memorable buildings — which he refers to as markers — for our perception of, and orientation within, urban spaces and structures. In this context, he speaks of the mental maps of familiar urban spaces and buildings that we draw in our mind's eye. These maps are not scale plans but records of our individual experience of urban space.

Fig.45:
The Guggenheim Museum in Bilbao, designed by Frank Gehry

as the Roman Colosseum, the Leaning Tower of Pisa and the Eiffel Tower. However, the significance of such buildings has increased enormously in recent times due to their presence in the media (on television, in advertising etc.) While all of them are remarkable for their size, they also share a specific expressiveness. The construction of the Guggenheim Museum in Bilbao – to return to the first example – has massively increased the number of tourists visiting the city.

THE GROUP

A group is an arrangement of buildings whose character is based more on inner compositional logic than external urban organization. Highly dense and organizationally complex groups are also referred to as clusters.

FORM AND SPATIAL STRUCTURE

Within a group, each element is attuned to the others and can only be understood in terms of its relationship to these other elements. › Fig. 46 As a rule, groups are based on an organizational principle according to which a whole is structured on the basis of interdependent parts. These are not combined additively as in the row › Chapter The row and are thus not arbitrarily extendable.

Manifold spatial configurations

The typological composition of groups can be very uniform, that is, limited to only a few types. However, the group can also combine a very diverse range of building types. It can include the different urban building blocks discussed in this publication (solitaires, ribbons, rows, courtyards and block fragments), which are arranged to create a formal and spatial tension. In these spatial configurations, concepts such as closeness, distance, integration and space (filled or empty) play an important role. Groups can include both open and closed building forms, and they

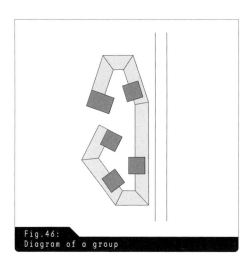

Fig.46:
Diagram of a group

are often organized around a common centre, an open space, a square, a green area or a spatial sequence of these elements. These spaces take on a particular significance for the identity of the group.

FORMATION OF URBAN SPACE

Dissociation from the urban context

The shared identity and recognizability of the group result in a more or less distinct dissociation from the surrounding urban context. In addition, groups form their own inner urban spaces and spatial sequences that assume different degrees of distinctiveness depending on the size and extensiveness of the group.

On the one hand, the individuality and recognizability of the group can allow inhabitants to identify with their residential and living environment. On the other, there is a danger that groups can become separate "islands" for different population groups, requirements, financial possibilities etc., which can undermine the socio-spatial coherence of the city. Such dangers and their consequences are clearly illustrated in the increasing prevalence of gated communities in large cities throughout the world.

> ⓝ

FUNCTIONS, ORIENTATION AND ACCESS

In many cases, groups consist of residential building projects, but they can have other functions, too. Examples include universities (where a self-contained campus constitutes a "city within the city"), hospitals and business parks. Mixed uses are possible but tend to be the exception because the group does not often allow adequate integration into the

ⓝ
\\ Note:
Gated communities are residential areas that are closed to general access and are guarded. Access is strictly regulated to protect the inhabitants from the dangers of the urban environment such as street crime and burglaries. Naturally, such exclusive residential areas create social segregation, but this is what their inhabitants desire. The concept of gated community can also be used in a figurative sense to refer to social and economic groups that seek to shield themselves from their environment.

surrounding urban environment. For this reason, a group needs to have a certain size if mixed uses are to be sustainable.

One advantage of the group – particularly the more complex cluster – lies in its structural density. However, this can produce orientation and lighting problems and, where residential units are too close together, a lack of privacy for the inhabitants.

Due to the importance of intermediate and internal spaces for the identity of the group, the use of cars in these areas is usually not permitted, or only to a limited extent. This creates attractive recreational and communal areas in the centre of the group, which are restricted to pedestrian and bicycle traffic. Parking spaces are located at ground level in the areas on the edge of the complex, or multi-storey car parks or underground garages can constructed, say, beneath the communal areas.

HISTORICAL EXAMPLES

From an urban-planning perspective, the Minoan Palace built in the first half of the second millennium BC on the island of Crete, and in particular the Palace of Knossos, can both be described as groups. › Fig. 47 Their complex spatial sequences and high-density created cluster-like structures whose interior orientation and labyrinthine organization ultimately provided the basis for the myth of Ariadne's thread. The interlocking residential quarters of cities in the Arab-Islamic world can also be described as groups or dense clusters.

However, the group is predominantly a product of the recent history of urban development, and social and communal considerations have played an important role in its development. We thus find groups in the workers' housing estates constructed at the end of the 19th century and in the designs of the garden city movement. Today, such projects are commonly seen as a viable means of saving costs and using space economically, and are often associated with an environmentally friendly and community-based approach to building. Groups and clusters are often collective building projects undertaken by construction collectives and building cooperatives. In this context, the construction of groups is not only seen as a way of reducing costs but also of providing a structural and urban expression of communal existence. In addition, there are of course projects financed by private investors and sold as condominiums or single-family houses.

Examples of groups and clusters of a particularly high architectural quality can be found in the work of the Swiss architectural firm Atelier 5.

Fig.47:
Layout of the Palace of Knossos on Crete

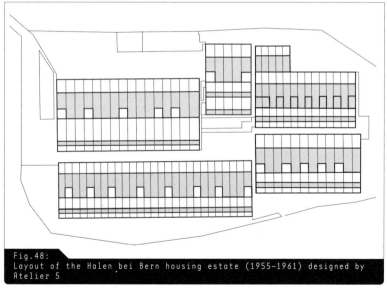

Fig.48:
Layout of the Halen bei Bern housing estate (1955–1961) designed by
Atelier 5

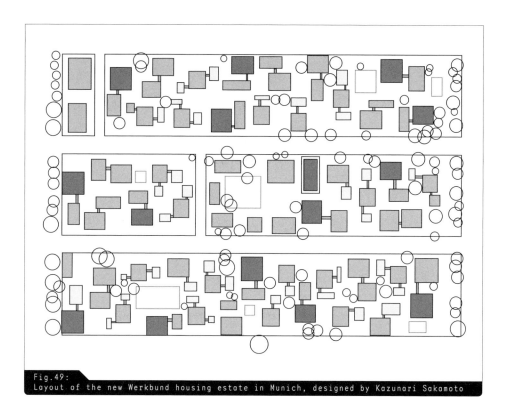

Fig.49:
Layout of the new Werkbund housing estate in Munich, designed by Kazunari Sakamoto

For years the firm has been developing housing projects as self-contained residential units that project a distinctive identity. A prime example is the Halen bei Bern estate built between 1955 and 1961. › Fig. 48 A more recent example can be seen in Japanese architect Kazunari Sakamoto's 2006 design for the Werkbund housing estate in Munich. The design is made up of a dense patchwork of solitaires of differing heights and a differentiated network of public, semi-public and private open areas. › Fig. 49

THE SHED

The shed is an urban building block similar to a solitaire, and may have a range of different sizes and dimensions. It is a characteristic phenomenon of the contemporary city and is notable for its conscious failure to establish any spatial or contextual reference. The term "shed" as an architectural concept was coined by Robert Venturi, Denise Scott Brown and Steven Izenour in their study Learning from Las Vegas, which was published in 1972.

Of all the urban building blocks referred to here, the shed is distinguished by its abnegation of external design. In this sense, it exhibits an eminently anti-urban character, since it consciously ignores the public space of the city. For a long time it was not perceived as an urban building block at all and remained an unnoticed aspect of industrial and commercial architecture.

However, the shed has now become a focus of interest for two reasons. First, its openness and adaptability to a diverse range of uses make

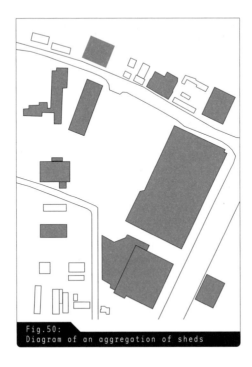

Fig.50:
Diagram of an aggregation of sheds

Fig.51:
Sheds in the contemporary urban landscape

it economically and structurally attractive. Second, its (non-)design has influenced the appearance of extensive areas of cities and their surroundings and thus the everyday living space of large numbers of people.

FORM AND SPATIAL STRUCTURE

In principle, sheds can assume any form that can be realized structurally, technically and economically. Its geometry and dimensions are also flexible, and shed structures can range from small factories to spacious shopping malls. › Fig. 50 However, the most distinctive characteristic of the shed is its lack of exterior design. The result is that it turns away from its surroundings. Its spatial disposition is derived exclusively from both technical requirements and interior organization and design, which, in contrast to the exterior, often place great importance on an attractive and customer-friendly environment. › Fig. 51

FORMATION OF URBAN SPACE

Sheds can be located anywhere. However, they significantly disrupt urban space because they fundamentally negate the architectural and urban design of streets and public spaces. As a rule, therefore, sheds are found on the outer peripheries of cities and the areas directly beyond them. Nevertheless, they have a significant influence on the everyday lives of a city's inhabitants.

The lack of exterior design is partly compensated for by billboards and large advertising areas, which are used as means to draw attention to the interior life of the shed and to attract customers. › Fig. 52 In some cases,

Fig.52:
Advertising pillars and billboards used to draw attention to the
interior functions of sheds

a particular corporate identity is developed by covering facade areas with recognizable patterns and fragmentary architectural elements.

FUNCTIONS, ORIENTATION AND ACCESS

Functional openness

Sheds can assume practically any function. Their form and spatial structure result from this functional openness and permanent convertibility. Sheds are usually surrounded by sufficient open space to accommodate large parking areas. In the rare case of higher visitor numbers and restricted space, for example in the inner city, additional sheds are erected as multi-storey car parks, or basement garages are constructed. › Fig. 53

Staging the city

In its interior, the appearance of the shed is often dramatically different. In the case of shopping centres, shed interiors are often designed to create the ambience and flair of an inner-city location. A prime example is Main-Taunus-Zentrum, which was constructed in the 1960s near Frankfurt as Europe's first shopping mall, and which can seen as representative of many such complexes. Inviting visitors to stroll and window-shop, it is organized around an inner arcade lined on both sides by shop windows and attractive displays. › Fig. 54 In order to enhance the "city feeling", widened areas resembling city squares have been integrated into the space, along with fountains and sculptures with an antiquated look. Shoppers can also

Fig.53:
Sheds as containers for parking
facilities

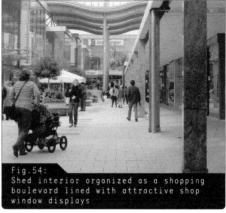

Fig.54:
Shed interior organized as a shopping
boulevard lined with attractive shop
window displays

relax in restaurants and ice cream parlours. Thus, the lack of exterior design and the mall's dissociation from the surrounding city is not reflected at all in the interior of the structure.

HISTORICAL EXAMPLES

Sheds in the sense used here first appeared in significant numbers in the period after World War II. Until this point, considerable importance was attached to the architectural design and structural integration of industrial facilities, transport infrastructure buildings and department stores. Notable examples include the buildings designed by Peter Behrens for AEG in Berlin prior to the World War I, Auguste Perret's Garage Rue Ponthieu (1905) in Paris, and the Tietz department store built by Bernhard Sehring on Berlin's Leipziger Strasse.

Abnegation of
external design

Economic advantages – and to a certain extent, the level of banality that crept into functionalist building – ultimately led to the practice of giving attention to the design of exterior surfaces only in those cases where utility buildings were exposed to customer traffic. Entrances and interior public areas were designed to have a representational function, while exterior surfaces, having no representational role, were neglected. Today the design of factories, multi-storey car parks, retail outlets and shopping malls often follows this logic.

Las Vegas

The best example of sheds like these can be found on the Strip in Las Vegas, where entertainment facilities, casinos, amusement arcades and hotels are based on the shed principle. Illuminated signs and billboards draw attention to the buildings and become surrogates for architectural and facade design, which are organized solely on the basis of their interior requirements. In their study of Las Vegas, Robert Venturi, Denise Scott-Brown and Steven Izenour refer to these structures as decorated sheds.

This development can be observed throughout the world. Ever greater areas of urban territory, in particular the peripheral areas around them, are changing drastically in appearance due to the influence of sheds. Since many everyday activities, particularly those that have to do with shopping and consumption, now take people into these areas, many spheres of life are being affected by this transformation, which is directed against the city and its public spaces.

Virtual worlds These changes are being reinforced by telematic developments and the increasing significance of virtual worlds. The architect Bernard Tschumi has argued that the Internet will decisively alter the design and appearance of our cities, citing as proof that he has not entered a bank since the advent of Internet banking. Shopping and interaction with administrative authorities are similarly being affected. Historical, representational architecture which once signalled from the outside how the building was used has become obsolete. A bank no longer has to look like a bank. If no one enters it anymore, it will probably suffice to place it in a shed.

IN CONCLUSION:
FROM BUILDING BLOCK OF THE CITY TO URBAN STRUCTURE

"Building cities involves designing groups and spaces with three-dimensional materials."

Albert Brinckmann (1908)

Once the characteristics and structures of individual urban building blocks have been identified, this knowledge can be applied to larger (urban) spatial contexts. It is only at the level of an urban neighbourhood or an entire city that the networks and interplay between the building blocks actually form the spaces in which we move, live and work every day. Although this book has presented these urban elements individually, it is important to study the diverse connections between them in order to understand the effect they have on the realities of urban existence. It is only in this way that the city can be comprehended as a complex system of spatial, functional and social interdependencies.

Urban building blocks play a central role in this system. As built structures they determine they way individual buildings are used, while indirectly influencing the intermediate spaces of the city – streets and access paths, squares and parks – in which public (and private) life takes place. The resulting spatial integration and forms of functional appropriation by residents and visitors also have an effect on the composition of the urban elements themselves.

Nevertheless, although a thorough knowledge of individual urban elements is essential, the city should be studied and designed as a whole. It is particularly important to bear this in mind when tackling the diverse challenges posed by the technological, demographic, socio-cultural and economic changes currently taking place in cities. Parts of cities are all too often planned and developed as functionally and socially isolated urban fragments. The "islands" that are thereby created may be optimal for certain uses and lifestyles, but other areas of the city may be left behind. In cases where the interplay of urban elements and the overall urban integration do not function, spatial and functional deficiencies often develop that rapidly start to exert an effect on economic and social spheres. The integration of the different parts of the city into an overall urban structure must therefore be a central concern of urban development.

As the 21st century begins, the sheer size of the agglomerations now forming extensive urbanized regions, international metropolises and mega-lopolises and the associated differentiation of their societies are naturally challenging the validity of long-established concepts and models. Nevertheless, many of the tasks involved in urban development have remained the same. Urban development has to create a physical identity and distinctive functional and social living spaces. It must include the design of intermediate spaces and, in particular, public spaces that are accessible to everyone at all times. It must search for a balance between public and private interests.

In this context, studying the building blocks of the city is a first step towards understanding the built urban structure in terms of its central significance as a physical living and cultural space and in an effort to develop it as such. It is on this basis that the frameworks and ultimately also the methods of city design need to be developed. Engaging in this process enables students to derive practical tips and insights that can help guide them in the task of conceptually planning urban living space. Further study and, of course, professional experience will lead them beyond these primary building blocks of the city to more complex arrangements of urban space. It is in such living and constantly changing contexts that the concepts introduced here will need to prove their worth.

APPENDIX

LITERATURE

Leonardo Benevolo: *The History of the City*, MIT Press, Cambridge (Mass.) 1980

Walter Benjamin: *The Arcades Project*, Belknap Press, Cambridge (Mass.) 1999

Chuihua Judy Chung, Jeffrey Inaba, Rem Koolhaas, Sze Tsung Leong: *Project on the City 2: Harvard Design School Guide to Shopping*, Harvard Graduate School of Design 2002

Friedrich Engels: *The Condition of the Working Class in England in 1844*, J. W. Lovell Company, New York 1887

Robert Fishman: *Bourgeois Utopias. The Rise and Fall of Suburbia*, Basic Books, New York 1987

Ebenezer Howard: *Tomorrow: A Peaceful Path to Real Reform*, London 1898

Le Corbusier: *The Athens Charter*, Grossman Publishers, New York 1973

Le Corbusier: *The Radiant City*, Orion Press, New York 1967

Le Corbusier: *Towards a new Architecture*, Dover Publications, New York 1986

Kevin Lynch: *The Image of the City*, Cambridge Technology Press, Cambridge (Mass.) 1960

Franz Oswald, Peter Baccini: *Netzstadt. Designing the Urban*, Birkhäuser, Basel 2003

Andrea Palladio: *Four Books on Architecture*, MIT Press, Cambridge (Mass.) 1997

Philippe Panerai, Jean Castex, Jean-Charles Depaule: *Urban Forms*, Architectural Press, Boston 2004

Aldo Rossi: *The Architecture of the City*, MIT Press, Cambridge (Mass.) 1982

Camillo Sitte: *The Art of Building Cities. City Building according to its Artistic Fundamentals*, Reinhold Publishing Corporation, New York 1945

Raymond Unwin: *Town Planning in Practice: An Introduction to the Art of Designing Cities and Suburbs*, T. F. Unwin, London 1909

Robert Venturi, Denise Scott Brown, Steven Izenour: *Learning from Las Vegas*, MIT Press, Cambridge (Mass.) 1972

THE AUTHORS

Thorsten Bürklin, Ph.D. in philosophy, M.S. in engineering, associate lecturer of urban planning and building science at the University of Applied Sciences in Frankfurt am Main, freelance architect in Karlsruhe.

Michael Peterek, Ph.D. in engineering, professor in the Department of Urban Planning and Design at the University of Applied Sciences in Frankfurt am Main, freelance urban planner in Frankfurt am Main.

Series editor: Bert Bielefeld
Conception: Bert Bielefeld, Annette Gref
Layout and Cover design: Muriel Comby
Translation into English: Adam Blauhut, Joseph
O'Donnell
English Copy editing: Monica Buckland

All drawings and illustrations from the authors'
archive.

Library of Congress Control Number: 2007932334

Bibliographic information published by the
German National Library
The German National Library lists this publication in the Deutsche Nationalbibliografie; detailed
bibliographic data are available on the Internet at
http://dnb.d-nb.de.

This book is also available in a German
(ISBN 978-3-7643-8459-3) and a French
(ISBN 978-3-7643-8461-6) language edition.

© 2008 Birkhäuser Verlag AG
Basel · Boston · Berlin
P.O. Box 133, CH-4010 Basel, Switzerland
Part of Springer Science+Business Media

Printed on acid-free paper produced from
chlorine-free pulp. TCF ∞
Printed in Germany

ISBN 978-3-7643-8460-9
9 8 7 6 5 4 3 2 1   www.birkhauser.ch

Also available from Birkhäuser:

Design

Basics Design and Living
Jan Krebs
978-3-7643-7647-5

Basics Design Ideas
Bert Bielefeld, Sebastian El khouli
978-3-7643-8112-7

Basics Design Methods
Kari Jormakka
978-3-7643-8463-0

Basics Materials
M. Hegger, H. Drexler, M. Zeumer
978-3-7643-7685-7

Fundamentals of Presentation

Basics CAD
Jan Krebs
978-3-7643-8109-7

Basics Modelbuilding
Alexander Schilling
978-3-7643-7649-9

Basics Technical Drawing
Bert Bielefeld, Isabella Skiba
978-3-7643-7644-4

Construction

Basics Facade Apertures
Roland Krippner, Florian Musso
978-3-7643-8466-1

Basics Loadbearing Systems
Alfred Meistermann
978-3-7643-8107-3

Basics Masonry Construction
Nils Kummer
978-3-7643-7645-1

Basics Roof Construction
Tanja Brotrück
978-3-7643-7683-3

Basics Timber Construction
Ludwig Steiger
978-3-7643-8102-8

Professional Practice

Basics Project Planning
Hartmut Klein
978-3-7643-8469-2

Basics Site Management
Lars-Philipp Rusch
978-3-7643-8104-2

Basics Tendering
Tim Brandt, Sebastian Th. Franssen
978-3-7643-8110-3